50 For the Love of Cheese Recipes

By: Kelly Johnson

Table of Contents

- Cheddar-Stuffed Jalapeño Poppers
- Three-Cheese Mac and Cheese
- Baked Brie with Cranberries and Walnuts
- Mozzarella-Stuffed Meatballs
- Parmesan-Crusted Chicken
- Gouda Grilled Cheese
- Blue Cheese Burger Sliders
- Feta and Spinach Stuffed Chicken
- Ricotta Pancakes
- Cream Cheese Stuffed French Toast
- Brie and Apple Quesadillas
- Cheesy Scalloped Potatoes
- Gruyère and Mushroom Tart
- Four-Cheese Lasagna
- Buffalo Chicken Dip with Cheddar
- Havarti and Ham Panini
- Cheese-Stuffed Garlic Knots

- White Cheddar Mashed Potatoes
- Cottage Cheese Pancakes
- Cheddar and Chive Biscuits
- Queso Fundido
- Swiss Cheese and Onion Soup
- Cheese-Stuffed Pretzel Bites
- Jalapeño Cheddar Cornbread
- Ricotta and Lemon Pasta
- Broccoli and Cheese Soup
- Smoked Mozzarella Flatbread
- Mac and Cheese Balls
- Cheesy Cauliflower Bake
- Baked Ziti with Mozzarella
- Cheddar Bacon Dip
- Gorgonzola and Pear Salad
- Cream Cheese Wontons
- Cheese-Stuffed Zucchini Boats
- Brie and Raspberry Crostini
- Cheddar and Ale Soup

- Ricotta and Spinach Stuffed Shells
- Nacho Cheese Chicken Tacos
- Provolone-Stuffed Burgers
- Pimento Cheese Spread
- Smoked Gouda Macaroni
- Cheese and Herb Frittata
- Cheesy Garlic Bread
- Blue Cheese and Fig Pizza
- Cream Cheese Brownies
- Mozzarella-Stuffed Peppers
- Brie and Bacon Puff Pastry Bites
- Parmesan Truffle Fries
- Caprese Grilled Cheese
- Cheddar Cheese Grits

Cheddar-Stuffed Jalapeño Poppers

Ingredients:

- 10 jalapeño peppers, halved and seeded
- 1 cup sharp cheddar cheese, shredded
- 4 oz cream cheese, softened
- 1/2 tsp garlic powder
- Salt and pepper to taste
- 1 cup panko breadcrumbs
- 2 eggs, beaten
- 1/2 cup flour
- Cooking spray or oil for baking

Instructions:

1. Preheat oven to 400°F (200°C).
2. In a bowl, mix cream cheese, cheddar, garlic powder, salt, and pepper.
3. Fill each jalapeño half with the cheese mixture.
4. Dredge each stuffed jalapeño in flour, dip in beaten egg, then coat in panko.
5. Place on a baking sheet and lightly spray with cooking oil.
6. Bake for 18–20 minutes until golden and bubbly. Serve hot.

Three-Cheese Mac and Cheese

Ingredients:

- 1 lb elbow macaroni
- 2 tbsp butter
- 2 tbsp all-purpose flour
- 2 cups milk
- 1 cup sharp cheddar, shredded
- 1 cup mozzarella, shredded
- 1/2 cup parmesan, grated
- 1/2 tsp paprika
- Salt and pepper to taste
- Optional: 1/2 cup panko for topping

Instructions:

1. Cook macaroni until al dente. Drain and set aside.
2. In a saucepan, melt butter over medium heat. Stir in flour to form a roux.
3. Slowly whisk in milk, cooking until thickened.
4. Stir in cheeses until melted. Add paprika, salt, and pepper.
5. Combine sauce with pasta and pour into a baking dish.
6. Top with panko if desired and broil until golden. Serve warm.

Baked Brie with Cranberries and Walnuts

Ingredients:

- 1 wheel of brie cheese (8 oz)
- 1/2 cup dried cranberries
- 1/3 cup chopped walnuts
- 2 tbsp honey
- 1 sheet puff pastry (optional)
- 1 egg, beaten (if using puff pastry)

Instructions:

1. Preheat oven to 375°F (190°C).
2. Place brie on a parchment-lined baking sheet or wrap in puff pastry.
3. Top with cranberries, walnuts, and drizzle with honey.
4. If using puff pastry, fold it over the brie and brush with egg wash.
5. Bake for 15–20 minutes until golden and gooey.
6. Let sit for 5 minutes, then serve with crackers or sliced baguette.

Mozzarella-Stuffed Meatballs

Ingredients:

- 1 lb ground beef or Italian sausage
- 1/4 cup breadcrumbs
- 1/4 cup grated parmesan
- 1 egg
- 1 tsp Italian seasoning
- Salt and pepper to taste
- 4 oz mozzarella, cut into ½-inch cubes
- Marinara sauce for serving

Instructions:

1. Preheat oven to 400°F (200°C).
2. In a bowl, combine meat, breadcrumbs, parmesan, egg, and seasoning.
3. Take a tablespoon of the meat mixture and flatten it.
4. Place a cube of mozzarella in the center and roll into a ball.
5. Place on a baking sheet and bake for 15–18 minutes.
6. Serve warm with marinara sauce.

Parmesan-Crusted Chicken

Ingredients:

- 4 boneless, skinless chicken breasts
- 1 cup grated Parmesan cheese
- 1 cup panko breadcrumbs
- 1 tsp garlic powder
- Salt and pepper to taste
- 2 eggs, beaten
- 1/2 cup flour
- Olive oil for cooking

Instructions:

1. Pound chicken to even thickness.
2. Mix Parmesan, breadcrumbs, garlic powder, salt, and pepper.
3. Dredge chicken in flour, dip in egg, then coat in Parmesan mixture.
4. Heat oil in skillet over medium heat and cook chicken 4–5 minutes per side until golden and cooked through.

Gouda Grilled Cheese

Ingredients:

- 8 slices sourdough or artisan bread
- 8 slices smoked Gouda
- 4 tbsp butter, softened
- Optional: caramelized onions or sliced tomatoes

Instructions:

1. Butter one side of each bread slice.
2. Place Gouda between unbuttered sides, adding extras if desired.
3. Grill on a skillet over medium heat until bread is golden and cheese is melted.

Blue Cheese Burger Sliders

Ingredients:

- 1 lb ground beef
- Salt and pepper to taste
- 1/2 cup crumbled blue cheese
- 8 slider buns
- Optional: arugula, caramelized onions, or aioli

Instructions:

1. Form beef into 8 small patties. Season with salt and pepper.
2. Grill or pan-fry until desired doneness.
3. Top each patty with blue cheese. Assemble on buns with toppings of choice.

Feta and Spinach Stuffed Chicken

Ingredients:

- 4 boneless, skinless chicken breasts
- 1 cup cooked spinach, drained
- 1/2 cup crumbled feta cheese
- 1 garlic clove, minced
- Salt and pepper to taste
- Olive oil for searing

Instructions:

1. Slice a pocket into each chicken breast.
2. Mix spinach, feta, garlic, salt, and pepper. Stuff into chicken.
3. Secure with toothpicks if needed. Sear in a skillet, then bake at 375°F (190°C) for 20 minutes.

Ricotta Pancakes

Ingredients:

- 1 cup ricotta cheese
- 3/4 cup milk
- 2 eggs, separated
- 1 cup flour
- 2 tbsp sugar
- 1 tsp baking powder
- Pinch of salt
- Butter for cooking

Instructions:

1. Mix ricotta, milk, and egg yolks.
2. In a separate bowl, whisk dry ingredients. Combine with wet mix.
3. Beat egg whites to soft peaks, then fold in gently.
4. Cook on a buttered skillet until golden on both sides.

Cream Cheese Stuffed French Toast

Ingredients:

- 8 slices brioche or thick bread
- 4 oz cream cheese, softened
- 2 tbsp powdered sugar
- 4 eggs
- 1/2 cup milk
- 1 tsp vanilla extract
- Butter for cooking

Instructions:

1. Mix cream cheese with powdered sugar and spread on 4 slices of bread. Top with remaining slices to form sandwiches.
2. Whisk eggs, milk, and vanilla. Dip sandwiches into the mixture.
3. Cook on a buttered skillet until golden and cooked through. Serve with syrup or fruit.

Brie and Apple Quesadillas

Ingredients:

- 4 flour tortillas
- 6 oz brie cheese, sliced
- 1 crisp apple, thinly sliced
- 1 tbsp honey (optional)
- Butter or oil for cooking

Instructions:

1. Layer brie and apple slices on half of each tortilla. Drizzle with honey if using.
2. Fold over and cook in a skillet with a little butter until cheese melts and tortilla is crisp. Slice and serve warm.

Cheesy Scalloped Potatoes

Ingredients:

- 3 lbs russet potatoes, thinly sliced
- 2 cups shredded cheddar cheese
- 1 cup heavy cream
- 1/2 cup milk
- 2 tbsp butter
- 2 tbsp flour
- 1 garlic clove, minced
- Salt and pepper to taste

Instructions:

1. Preheat oven to 375°F (190°C).
2. Make a roux with butter, garlic, and flour. Slowly whisk in cream and milk. Stir in cheese until melted.
3. Layer potatoes in a greased baking dish, pouring sauce over each layer.
4. Cover and bake for 40 minutes. Uncover and bake an additional 15–20 minutes until golden and bubbly.

Gruyère and Mushroom Tart

Ingredients:

- 1 sheet puff pastry, thawed
- 1 cup Gruyère cheese, shredded
- 1 cup mushrooms, sliced
- 1 small onion, sliced
- 1 tbsp olive oil
- 1 tsp thyme
- Salt and pepper to taste

Instructions:

1. Preheat oven to 400°F (200°C).
2. Sauté mushrooms and onions with oil, thyme, salt, and pepper.
3. Roll out pastry on a baking sheet. Layer Gruyère, then mushroom mixture.
4. Bake for 20–25 minutes until puffed and golden.

Four-Cheese Lasagna

Ingredients:

- 9 lasagna noodles
- 2 cups marinara sauce
- 1 cup ricotta cheese
- 1 cup mozzarella cheese, shredded
- 1 cup provolone cheese, shredded
- 1/2 cup parmesan cheese, grated
- 1 egg
- Salt, pepper, and Italian seasoning to taste

Instructions:

1. Preheat oven to 375°F (190°C). Cook noodles as directed.
2. Mix ricotta with egg, salt, pepper, and seasoning.
3. Layer sauce, noodles, ricotta mix, and cheeses in a 9x13 baking dish. Repeat layers.
4. Top with remaining cheese. Cover and bake for 30 minutes, then uncover and bake 10 more until bubbly.

Buffalo Chicken Dip with Cheddar

Ingredients:

- 2 cups shredded cooked chicken
- 8 oz cream cheese, softened
- 1/2 cup buffalo wing sauce
- 1 cup shredded cheddar cheese
- 1/2 cup ranch or blue cheese dressing
- Optional: green onions or extra cheese for topping

Instructions:

1. Preheat oven to 375°F (190°C).
2. Mix all ingredients in a bowl until well combined.
3. Spread into a baking dish and bake for 20 minutes, or until bubbly.
4. Top with extra cheese or green onions and serve with chips or celery sticks.

Havarti and Ham Panini

Ingredients:

- 8 slices rustic bread
- 8 slices Havarti cheese
- 8 slices deli ham
- 2 tbsp Dijon mustard
- Butter for grilling

Instructions:

1. Spread mustard on 4 slices of bread.
2. Layer with ham and cheese, then top with remaining bread.
3. Butter outsides and grill in a panini press or skillet until golden and melty.

Cheese-Stuffed Garlic Knots

Ingredients:

- 1 can pizza dough
- 4 oz mozzarella, cubed
- 2 tbsp butter
- 1 tsp garlic powder
- 1 tsp parsley
- Salt to taste

Instructions:

1. Preheat oven to 400°F (200°C).
2. Cut dough into strips, wrap around a cube of cheese, and tie into knots.
3. Bake for 10–12 minutes until golden.
4. Brush with melted butter mixed with garlic powder, parsley, and salt.

White Cheddar Mashed Potatoes

Ingredients:

- 2 lbs Yukon Gold potatoes, peeled and cubed
- 1/2 cup milk
- 1/4 cup butter
- 1 cup shredded white cheddar
- Salt and pepper to taste

Instructions:

1. Boil potatoes until tender, then drain.
2. Mash with milk, butter, and cheese until creamy.
3. Season with salt and pepper. Serve warm.

Cottage Cheese Pancakes

Ingredients:

- 1 cup cottage cheese
- 3 eggs
- 1/2 cup flour
- 1/4 tsp salt
- 1/2 tsp baking powder
- Butter for cooking

Instructions:

1. Whisk together all ingredients until combined.
2. Heat butter on a skillet and pour in batter by the spoonful.
3. Cook until golden on each side. Serve with fruit or syrup.

Cheddar and Chive Biscuits

Ingredients:

- 2 cups flour
- 1 tbsp baking powder
- 1/2 tsp salt
- 1/2 cup cold butter, cubed
- 1 cup shredded cheddar
- 1/4 cup chopped chives
- 3/4 cup milk

Instructions:

1. Preheat oven to 425°F (220°C).
2. Mix flour, baking powder, and salt. Cut in butter.
3. Stir in cheese, chives, and milk until just combined.
4. Drop onto a baking sheet and bake 12–15 minutes.

Queso Fundido

Ingredients:

- 2 cups shredded Oaxaca or Monterey Jack cheese
- 1/2 cup cooked chorizo
- 1 small onion, diced
- 1 jalapeño, chopped
- Tortillas or chips for serving

Instructions:

1. Preheat oven to 375°F (190°C).
2. Sauté onion, jalapeño, and chorizo in a skillet.
3. Stir in cheese and transfer skillet to oven.
4. Bake until cheese is melted and bubbly. Serve hot.

Swiss Cheese and Onion Soup

Ingredients:

- 4 large onions, thinly sliced
- 2 tbsp butter
- 1 tbsp flour
- 6 cups beef broth
- 1 tsp thyme
- Salt and pepper to taste
- Baguette slices
- 1 cup shredded Swiss cheese

Instructions:

1. Cook onions in butter until deeply caramelized.
2. Stir in flour, then broth and thyme. Simmer for 30 minutes.
3. Top with toasted baguette slices and Swiss cheese. Broil until bubbly.

Cheese-Stuffed Pretzel Bites

Ingredients:

- 1 can refrigerated pizza dough
- 4 oz cheddar, cubed
- 1/4 cup baking soda
- 1 egg, beaten
- Coarse salt

Instructions:

1. Preheat oven to 425°F (220°C).
2. Cut dough into small pieces, wrap around cheese cubes.
3. Boil water with baking soda. Dip bites in for 30 seconds.
4. Place on baking sheet, brush with egg, sprinkle with salt.
5. Bake 12–15 minutes until golden.

Jalapeño Cheddar Cornbread

Ingredients:

- 1 cup cornmeal
- 1 cup flour
- 1 tbsp sugar
- 1 tbsp baking powder
- 1/2 tsp salt
- 1 cup milk
- 1 egg
- 1/4 cup melted butter
- 1 cup shredded cheddar
- 1–2 jalapeños, diced

Instructions:

1. Preheat oven to 400°F (200°C).
2. Mix dry ingredients in one bowl and wet ingredients in another.
3. Combine, then fold in cheese and jalapeños.
4. Pour into a greased pan and bake for 20–25 minutes.

Ricotta and Lemon Pasta

Ingredients:

- 12 oz pasta (like linguine or penne)
- 1 cup ricotta cheese
- Zest and juice of 1 lemon
- 1/4 cup grated parmesan
- Salt, pepper, and olive oil
- Optional: basil or parsley

Instructions:

1. Cook pasta, reserving 1/2 cup of the water.
2. Mix ricotta, lemon zest, juice, parmesan, salt, pepper, and a drizzle of olive oil.
3. Toss pasta with ricotta mixture, adding reserved water as needed for creaminess.
4. Garnish with herbs if desired.

Broccoli and Cheese Soup

Ingredients:

- 4 cups broccoli florets
- 1 small onion, diced
- 2 cloves garlic, minced
- 2 tbsp butter
- 2 tbsp flour
- 2 cups milk
- 2 cups chicken or vegetable broth
- 2 cups shredded cheddar
- Salt and pepper to taste

Instructions:

1. Sauté onion and garlic in butter. Stir in flour and cook 1–2 minutes.
2. Gradually add milk and broth, whisking to avoid lumps.
3. Add broccoli, simmer 15 minutes.
4. Stir in cheddar and blend partially (or fully) if desired. Season and serve warm.

Smoked Mozzarella Flatbread

Ingredients:

- 2 flatbreads or naan
- 1 cup smoked mozzarella, shredded
- 1/2 cup cherry tomatoes, halved
- 1/4 cup fresh basil, chopped
- Olive oil
- Salt and pepper

Instructions:

1. Preheat oven to 425°F (220°C).
2. Brush flatbreads with olive oil, top with cheese and tomatoes.
3. Bake 8–10 minutes or until crisp.
4. Sprinkle with basil, salt, and pepper before serving.

Mac and Cheese Balls

Ingredients:

- 2 cups cooked mac and cheese, chilled
- 1 cup breadcrumbs
- 1/2 cup flour
- 2 eggs, beaten
- Oil for frying

Instructions:

1. Roll chilled mac and cheese into balls.
2. Dredge in flour, dip in egg, and coat with breadcrumbs.
3. Fry in hot oil until golden brown.
4. Drain on paper towels and serve hot.

Cheesy Cauliflower Bake

Ingredients:

- 1 large head cauliflower, cut into florets
- 1 cup shredded cheddar
- 1/2 cup sour cream
- 1/4 cup milk
- 1 tsp garlic powder
- Salt and pepper

Instructions:

1. Steam or boil cauliflower until just tender.
2. Mix with sour cream, milk, cheese, and seasonings.
3. Transfer to a baking dish and bake at 375°F (190°C) for 20–25 minutes until bubbly and golden.

Baked Ziti with Mozzarella

Ingredients:

- 1 lb ziti pasta
- 2 cups marinara sauce
- 1 cup ricotta cheese
- 1 egg
- 2 cups shredded mozzarella
- 1/2 cup grated parmesan
- Salt, pepper, and basil

Instructions:

1. Preheat oven to 375°F (190°C).
2. Cook pasta, then mix with sauce.
3. Combine ricotta, egg, and seasoning. Layer pasta, ricotta mix, and mozzarella in a dish.
4. Top with parmesan and bake 30 minutes.

Cheddar Bacon Dip

Ingredients:

- 8 oz cream cheese, softened
- 1 cup shredded cheddar
- 1/2 cup sour cream
- 1/4 cup cooked crumbled bacon
- 2 green onions, sliced

Instructions:

1. Mix cream cheese, sour cream, cheddar, and most of the bacon and green onions.
2. Spread in a dish and bake at 350°F (175°C) for 15 minutes.
3. Garnish with remaining bacon and onions. Serve with chips or veggies.

Gorgonzola and Pear Salad

Ingredients:

- 4 cups mixed greens
- 1 ripe pear, sliced
- 1/4 cup crumbled gorgonzola
- 1/4 cup candied pecans or walnuts
- Balsamic glaze or vinaigrette

Instructions:

1. Toss greens, pears, cheese, and nuts in a bowl.
2. Drizzle with balsamic and serve immediately.

Cream Cheese Wontons

Ingredients:

- 8 oz cream cheese, softened
- 2 green onions, chopped
- 20 wonton wrappers
- Oil for frying

Instructions:

1. Mix cream cheese and green onions.
2. Place 1 tsp filling in each wrapper, seal edges with water.
3. Fry until golden and crispy. Serve with sweet chili sauce.

Cheese-Stuffed Zucchini Boats

Ingredients:

- 3 medium zucchinis, halved lengthwise and scooped
- 1 cup ricotta cheese
- 1/2 cup mozzarella, shredded
- 1/4 cup parmesan
- 1 egg
- Salt, pepper, Italian seasoning

Instructions:

1. Preheat oven to 375°F (190°C).
2. Mix cheeses, egg, and seasonings.
3. Spoon mixture into zucchini halves.
4. Bake for 25 minutes or until golden and tender.

Brie and Raspberry Crostini

Ingredients:

- 1 baguette, sliced
- 6 oz brie, sliced
- 1/2 cup raspberry preserves or fresh raspberries
- Optional: fresh thyme or mint

Instructions:

1. Toast baguette slices lightly.
2. Top with brie and a dollop of preserves.
3. Broil briefly until cheese melts.
4. Garnish with herbs if using and serve warm.

Cheddar and Ale Soup

Ingredients:

- 2 tbsp butter
- 1 small onion, diced
- 2 cloves garlic, minced
- 2 tbsp flour
- 1 cup ale or light beer
- 2 cups chicken broth
- 1 cup heavy cream
- 2 cups sharp cheddar, shredded
- Salt, pepper, and paprika

Instructions:

1. Sauté onion and garlic in butter until soft.
2. Stir in flour and cook for 1 minute.
3. Slowly whisk in ale and broth. Simmer 10 minutes.
4. Add cream and cheese. Stir until smooth. Season to taste.

Ricotta and Spinach Stuffed Shells

Ingredients:

- 20 jumbo pasta shells
- 1 ½ cups ricotta cheese
- 1 cup cooked spinach, squeezed dry
- 1 egg
- 1 cup mozzarella, shredded
- 2 cups marinara sauce
- 1/4 cup parmesan
- Salt, pepper, and basil

Instructions:

1. Preheat oven to 375°F (190°C).
2. Cook shells until al dente. Mix ricotta, spinach, egg, mozzarella, salt, and pepper.
3. Fill each shell and place in a baking dish with sauce.
4. Top with parmesan and bake 25 minutes.

Nacho Cheese Chicken Tacos

Ingredients:

- 2 cups shredded cooked chicken
- 1/2 cup nacho cheese sauce
- 8 taco shells
- Toppings: shredded lettuce, tomato, jalapeños, sour cream

Instructions:

1. Warm chicken and mix with cheese sauce.
2. Spoon into taco shells and load with toppings.
3. Serve hot for cheesy taco goodness.

Provolone-Stuffed Burgers

Ingredients:

- 1 lb ground beef
- 4 slices provolone, folded
- Salt, pepper, garlic powder
- Burger buns and toppings

Instructions:

1. Divide beef into 8 thin patties.
2. Sandwich cheese between 2 patties, sealing edges.
3. Season and grill or pan-fry until cooked through.
4. Serve on buns with your favorite toppings.

Pimento Cheese Spread

Ingredients:

- 2 cups shredded sharp cheddar
- 4 oz cream cheese, softened
- 1/2 cup mayonnaise
- 1/4 cup chopped pimentos
- Salt, pepper, cayenne

Instructions:

1. Blend everything until creamy and combined.
2. Chill before serving. Great on crackers, sandwiches, or burgers.

Smoked Gouda Macaroni

Ingredients:

- 12 oz pasta
- 2 tbsp butter
- 2 tbsp flour
- 2 cups milk
- 2 cups shredded smoked gouda
- Salt, pepper, paprika

Instructions:

1. Cook pasta and set aside.
2. Make a roux with butter and flour, then whisk in milk.
3. Stir in cheese until melted. Season and toss with pasta.

Cheese and Herb Frittata

Ingredients:

- 6 eggs
- 1/4 cup milk
- 1 cup shredded cheese (cheddar, mozzarella, etc.)
- 1/4 cup chopped herbs (parsley, chives, basil)
- Salt and pepper

Instructions:

1. Preheat oven to 375°F (190°C).
2. Whisk eggs, milk, cheese, herbs, and seasoning.
3. Pour into greased ovenproof skillet.
4. Cook on stovetop 2–3 minutes, then bake 10–12 minutes until set.

Cheesy Garlic Bread

Ingredients:

- 1 loaf French bread
- 1/2 cup butter, softened
- 3 cloves garlic, minced
- 1 cup mozzarella, shredded
- 1/4 cup parmesan
- Parsley for garnish

Instructions:

1. Preheat oven to 400°F (200°C).
2. Mix butter and garlic, spread on halved bread.
3. Top with cheeses and bake 10 minutes or until bubbly.
4. Garnish with parsley and slice to serve.

Blue Cheese and Fig Pizza

Ingredients:

- 1 pizza dough
- 1/2 cup fig jam or fresh figs, sliced
- 1 cup mozzarella
- 1/4 cup crumbled blue cheese
- Optional: arugula and balsamic glaze

Instructions:

1. Preheat oven to 475°F (245°C).
2. Spread fig jam on dough, add mozzarella and blue cheese.
3. Bake for 10–12 minutes.
4. Top with arugula and balsamic if desired.

Cream Cheese Brownies

Ingredients:

- 1 box brownie mix (plus ingredients on box)
- 8 oz cream cheese, softened
- 1/4 cup sugar
- 1 egg
- 1/2 tsp vanilla

Instructions:

1. Prepare brownie batter and pour into greased pan.
2. Beat cream cheese, sugar, egg, and vanilla.
3. Dollop over brownie batter and swirl with a knife.
4. Bake according to brownie box directions. Cool and cut.

Mozzarella-Stuffed Peppers

Ingredients:

- 4 bell peppers, halved and seeded
- 1 ½ cups cooked rice or quinoa
- 1 cup shredded mozzarella
- 1/2 cup marinara sauce
- 1/4 cup chopped basil
- Salt and pepper

Instructions:

1. Preheat oven to 375°F (190°C).
2. Mix rice, mozzarella, marinara, basil, salt, and pepper.
3. Fill pepper halves with mixture and place in a baking dish.
4. Cover with foil and bake 30 minutes. Remove foil and bake 10 more minutes until cheese is bubbly.

Brie and Bacon Puff Pastry Bites

Ingredients:

- 1 sheet puff pastry, thawed
- 4 oz brie, cubed
- 4 slices cooked bacon, chopped
- 1/4 cup fig jam or honey
- 1 egg, beaten

Instructions:

1. Preheat oven to 400°F (200°C).
2. Cut puff pastry into 12 squares and place in mini muffin tins.
3. Add a piece of brie, a bit of jam, and bacon to each.
4. Brush edges with egg wash and bake 15 minutes until golden.

Parmesan Truffle Fries

Ingredients:

- 4 large russet potatoes, cut into fries
- 2 tbsp olive oil
- 1 tbsp truffle oil
- 1/3 cup grated parmesan
- Salt and pepper
- Chopped parsley (optional)

Instructions:

1. Preheat oven to 425°F (220°C).
2. Toss fries with olive oil, salt, and pepper.
3. Bake for 30–35 minutes, flipping halfway.
4. Drizzle with truffle oil and sprinkle with parmesan and parsley before serving.

Caprese Grilled Cheese

Ingredients:

- 4 slices sourdough bread
- 4 slices mozzarella
- 1 tomato, sliced
- Fresh basil leaves
- Balsamic glaze
- Butter

Instructions:

1. Butter bread and layer with mozzarella, tomato, basil, and a drizzle of balsamic.
2. Cook in a skillet over medium heat until golden and cheese is melted, flipping once.
3. Slice and serve hot.

Cheddar Cheese Grits

Ingredients:

- 1 cup stone-ground grits
- 4 cups water or milk (or a combo)
- 1 cup sharp cheddar, shredded
- 2 tbsp butter
- Salt and pepper

Instructions:

1. Bring liquid to a boil, whisk in grits, reduce heat, and simmer until thick (about 20–25 minutes), stirring often.
2. Stir in butter, cheese, salt, and pepper.
3. Serve hot—great as a base for shrimp or eggs.

www.ingramcontent.com/pod-product-compliance
Lightning Source LLC
LaVergne TN
LVHW061950070526
838199LV00060B/4063